Devil's LANE

Devil's LANE

VIVIAN SHIPLEY

Negative Capability Press
Mobile, Alabama

Copyright © 1996 Vivian Shipley

FIRST EDITION

All rights reserved

DESIGNED BY BARBARA WERDEN

ISBN: 0-942544-52-8

Library of Congress Catalogue Card Number 96-067115

The author would like to thank the editors of the following periodicals in which these poems first appeared: *The Nebraska Review:* "This Is Bluegrass Country," "Alice Todd, Outside Somerset, Kentucky"; *The American Scholar:* "Black Hole"; *Riverrun:* "And We Are Here as On a Darkling Plain"; *Indiana Review:* "Three Legged Tracks"; *Gulf Coast:* "Killing Frost"; *Whiskey Island Magazine:* "White Chickens"; *Southern Poetry Review:* "A Keeper"; *The Windless Orchard:* "Praying You're Are Asleep"; *The Texas Review:* "How Sweet the Sound"; *Elk River Review:* "With a Hand on the Limb"; *The Florida Review:* "No Creel Limit"; *Northeast Corridor:* "Our Museum Selves"; *Slant:* "Carolyn Forche's in El Salvador"; *Birmingham Poetry Review:* "Christine, at Night, I Tired; Early Morning, I. . ."; *Poet Lore:* "Monroe: Sweetheart of the Month," "Our Bodies, Arms of a Weathervane Pointing North and South"; *Flint Hills Review:* "Star"; *Quarterly West:* "Moonshine"; *Negative Capability:* "Here's Looking at You, Kid," "Hitchhiking Mass Pike"; *The Wisconsin Review:* "We Were Wrong, Terribly Wrong," "When Your Number's Up"; *Ascent:* "How to Find George Sterling: Revise the Canon"; *Hampden Sydney Review:* "Why I Fish"; *The Journal:* "Action News, Channel Eight," "Horse Breath Winter"; *The Dominion Review:* "Results of the Blood Test"; *New Letters:* "Ice Bites Inward"; *The MacGuffin:* "An Old Husband's Tale"; *Red Brick Review:* "As if Corn Could Invent Itself"; *Chiron Review:* "Devil's Lane"; *Kestrel:* "Four Dollars Bought a Round Trip on the Sky Lift to the Top"; *Nimrod:* "No Six Pounders," "Night Fishing at Morgan Point"; *Painted Bride Quarterly:* "Unnatural"; *Hayden's Ferry Review:* "Stony Creek Granite"; *Yemassee:* "Soon, Soon."

Contents

This Is Bluegrass Country   1
Alice Todd, Outside Somerset, Kentucky   2
Black Hole   3
And We Are Here as on a Darkling Plain   5
Three Legged Tracks   6
Killing Frost   9
White Chickens   11
A Keeper   12
Praying You Are Asleep   14
How Sweet the Sound   15
With a Hand on the Limb   17
No Creel Limit   19
Our Museum Selves   20
Carolyn Forche's in El Salvador   22
Christine, at Night, I Tired; Early Morning, I . . .   23
Monroe: Sweetheart of the Month   25
Star   26
Outside the Rainbow   29
Moonshine   30
Here's Looking at You, Kid   32
Hitchhiking Mass. Pike   33
Week Four: Story About Another Person   34
We Were Wrong, Terribly Wrong   36
Don't Buy *The New Haven Register*   38
How to Find George Sterling: Revise the Canon   39
Why I Fish   41
Am Braighe   43
Action News, Channel Eight   45
Results of the Blood Test   46
Color   48

Our Bodies, Arms of a Weathervane Pointing North and South   49
When Your Number's Up   52
Ice Bites Inward   53
Like a Peacock, or So Folks Said   54
The Obituary   56
An Old Husband's Tale   58
A Rose by Any Other Name Would Smell as Sweet   59
As If Corn Could Invent Itself   64
Devil's Lane   65
Circling Above You   67
Four Dollars Bought a Round Trip on the Sky Lift to the Top   68
Act V, Scene iii   71
There Were the Signs You Had Shown Me: 72
Catfishing in Cumberland Lake   74
No Six Pounders   77
Unnatural   78
Night Fishing at Morgan Point   80
No Ark   82
Horse Breath Winter   83
Stony Creek Granite   84
Soon, Soon   86
The Stepfather   87

Devil's LANE

For Ed

This Is Bluegrass Country

> *My object in living is to unite*
> ROBERT FROST

land that has never been an Iroquois battleground
so we won't even bother poking around for arrowheads

but there's a story I can recite for you about the path
we walk on. Farmers who own the fields on either side

can't agree on a common boundary for economy
and each has built a creosote fence leaving a passage

called Devil's Lane. Standing between pastures freshly
mown, the grass green as our uncoached kisses,

my arms are bare to a heat that predicts lightning. Should
it strike, you remind me, don't cower under a tree;

go stand in the open. Leaning on a post, you compare
our love to gauge blocks, machine shop measures

that don't need anything except their trueness to keep
them together. That day, our words were not the offenses

we would shape and hang up to dry, preserved cardboard
pieces of the African puzzle you glued on a mat for framing.

Alice Todd, Outside Somerset, Kentucky

Born at the head of Rough Creek
in half-dovetailed logs daubed with mud,
my mother claimed one window to watch
two woodpeckers clash for a nesting cavity
in a dead oak: one golden shafted flicker,
the other she couldn't name, blue-black
and white with a ruby velvet head. Even
as a girl, she chased out dirt in that house;
odds were against her. She counted white-eyed
vireo, grosbeak colored the lapis lazuli I dreamed
reading Robert Browning's bishop order his tomb.
I would not marry back to naked barnyard.

Ocean was in early morning fog resting heavy
on ridges in Hardin County; diamonds in frost
ribbing a blackberry bush's leaf. Building castles
in damp yellow sand, my bare foot shaped a tunnel
where water could escape and it didn't cave in as I
slowly pulled out. Fearing the fall into the creek full
of crawdads, hornyheads and jackfish, I'd ignore
the log, hang on the rope over the swinging bridge.

I cannot string those boards together, bruise
myself a crossing for the quiet smell of ashes
or a drink, my hands cupped under the clear cold spring
where the creek began its long journey to South Fork
to join North Fork then create the Kentucky River
outside Beattyville, a town my mother never saw.
When traps set by furriers on Rough Creek's banks
snapped, there was no way to escape. To get free, a fox
or muskrat had to gnaw away a leg for the creek to swallow.

Black Hole

Was your mind vacant like Harlan county mine shafts or dark
as the lake in Mammoth Cave when the tour guide flicked

off light? I grabbed for you, Uncle, but you leaned back
in the boat's seat. Your silence taunts me; I can't let go

of the quarrel you would not join in last summer when I blurted
out I couldn't help it you weren't a father, that I was not the boy

you wanted. Showing how much science I had learned anyway,
I repeated a lecture about black holes, dense clumps of mass

in outer space with a gravitational force so strong that stars,
meteors, gas clouds and even light were sucked in as I was

by hope of even a nod from you. You were fingering the top
you'd whittled but I continued right on hoping to startle you

with a list of statistics, how the hole might contain well over
two billion suns, that Albert Einstein predicted them in 1915

even though he had no way of proving the identity of one
until the Hubble Space Telescope could spot the distant whirlpools

of stars as they were snuffed out. Certain as the scientists
of density I couldn't see, sure there must be a black hole behind

leathered furrows about your eyes, I tried to settle my hook
with talk of *Star Trek* and how time and space could be stretched,

twisted, torn or looped to take trips into other eras and dimensions.
Not even waiting to hear the grand finale, how the only way

to escape a black hole was to travel faster than the speed
of light, you called out to Uncle Paul, in from the back field,

that, finally, you had figured out how to pick out Queenie's
hunting mouth from her treed mouth. When you slumped

gray faced over the tractor, you made no sound, left no word
for me resting on the tip of your tongue like communion cubes

before the preacher gives the congregation a signal to swallow
the bread, transformed into flesh by the human need for love.

And We Are Here as on a Darkling Plain

This June afternoon, Matthew Arnold's line
from *Dover Beach* can't obliterate ripe
brie or casaba melon on the tine
of my fork. Red pistachios I wipe
off of my fingers rival the full glass
of burgundy for color splashed on back
drops of Long Island Sound. Waves start to mass
off rocks of Morgan Point. There is no lack
of water, of sand to streak. There will be
no end but such perspective undoes life.
I close the book on white cliffs, on the sea
and its *grating roar of pebbles*. Their strife
is blocked when my son Matthew of six full
months puts his mouth onto my breast to pull.

Three Legged Tracks

> *I go stumbling (head turned) back to my origins*
> DENISE LEVERTOV

Humiliated, I take aim with the camera and click. I'll show
my father how he looks in four shirts and that hat, pants hitched
up, standing out in the rain feeding sparrows as if they were
chickens he taught me how to hypnotize. My mother would have
called him a caution, a ring tailed caution. A baby sitter next door
wouldn't let him in, called last night to warn me about the character
wandering around. Tact, concern for his safety don't work; he

tells me he can get about just fine in the dark, has owl's blood;
some dogs just keep their noses to the ground and see nothing
above their heads but not him. Kiss me, he says. Taste wildness
of survivors: ginseng, pawpaws, arrowood pods, root of ginger.
We pitch horseshoes on Saturdays, he can't see the stake but
his arm remembers how to pitch ringers like he used to on his farm.
In bib overalls wiped with cow manure, his big hands jutted out

rubbing denim cuffs. My father could sit without thinking, moving
just to wipe his mouth, snuffing and spitting through sagging
gums; his teeth were set on a shelf. Endless, days were powdered
dirt clouded by my barefeet running for Nellie, a plow horse who
knew to puff her stomach, keep my saddle loose when she inhaled.
Kick her so the strap will stay, my father would shout. Bend
to cinch the girth but dodge teeth that will aim for a shoulder.

January mornings, I watched as he warmed the bit in his palm
to keep it from sticking to Snip's mouth, mutilating his tongue.
Tail hair could be used to restring a fiddle so we could play along
with the Opry, Hank Snow saying: *Good night. Good luck. Good
health. And may the good Lord always be proud of you.* Hank

should have substituted *daughter* for *lord* to teach me a lesson
but I didn't need a dictionary to learn my father's vocabulary list:

i. *seasons*: setting was done by Decoration Day, cutting
Labor Day weekend and stripping by Thanksgiving.

ii. *discipline*: tight bales.

iii. *foresight*: a few hands of tobacco, dry and stripped
from stems, crumbled into a nail keg to flesh out
Brown Mule chewing tobacco, Duke's Mixture.

iv. *awaken*: how to tease an appetite in steel by using the
whetstone to sharpen a blade for cutting hay.

v. *luxury:* cutting out the hearts of Rocky Ford watermelons
lying out in the field and eating them by the moonlight.

vi. *pride:* frying eggs for white bread when men would
come knocking at the back door, looking for work.

vii. *cruelty:* torching spiders

viii. *contentment*: old rams butting each other like aging
lovers.

ix. *survival:* holding a rifle light as cottonwood. Coming
up real slow, not aiming too long, shooting fast.

x. *evasion:* jumping pools of tobacco juice spit by boys
lining Elizabethtown's courthouse square each Saturday.

These ten words stay with me, fossiled like limestone stacked
into fences until arthritic hands gave in and my uncle came
back home to help stretch and staple wire to the trees. Trunks

7

have grown around barbs embedded in scarred bark and the pond
by the back barn has filled with silt of years, too shallow now
for breath. My father used to make me sit on the edge and let
the bluegill take the bobber and run before I set the hook

but the last time we fished, he kept reeling in and moving his bait
as if impatient for the strike to come. Leading him in by the arm
from my backyard, I let him talk on about how he has to get up
before sunrise to clean up the plow so he can push it to break fields
into ruts. While planting, my father always had a stalk of grass
thrusting through brown lips and knew all about appetite of dirt
for seed corn he flung as if he was scattering ashes into the earth.

Killing Frost

Self-righteous with stories of the sow that ate her young in a sty
    plastered with dung, my father said pigs were
intelligent — that when she was eating, she knew. I could see they
    were vicious right until a sharp blow on the back
of the head with an axe. Their slaughter was never the dull routine

of cattle who die without making sounds. Like blackberry thorns,
    hog squeals were hard to pull out, unlike a knife
plunged to jugular at Aunt Hazel's command, *Stick 'im right*
    in th' goozle 'ere. Sanctimonious is how I'd describe
us as a stake sharpened at both ends was put between tendons

and front feet to hold the carcass. We hoisted the hog full length
    into a barrel of boiling water to get bristles out.
The head was twisted off and brains were scooped out to fry
    with eggs for breakfast. Finally, there was real
satisfaction, a climax: one long cut down the belly spilled the red,

shining like ebony. Warmed by exhaust from a Ford tractor, we'd
    trade techniques: hogs should be killed late November
on the full moon or just about. While the moon waned, meat would
    shrink with too much lard and in new moon, there
wouldn't be enough grease. A slice in a pan would puff up and spit

right in your eye just like an adder. Hogs we didn't kill were taken
    on Saturday to Elizabethtown but only when the moon
was growing so the meat would hold water and weigh more. Eating
    held significance, a reputation was made on curing
ham. Doc Hall Purtle used five pounds of salt for a two hundred

pound hog. My father liked eight pounds per hundred mixed
    with black and red pepper and at least a quart
of molasses. Neighbors buried hams in bushels of corn or hickory

ash but ours were wrapped in layers of gauze
with red stain seeping through like a shroud. Swinging on hooks,

shoulders hung aloft until the peach trees bloomed. Then hams
were put flat side down on bare ground. Cured
for two years, the unveiling was a ritual until we reached the hard
brown fat that was far too tempting to use as an altar
for kneeling. Thirty years later, I read New Haven, Connecticut

on *The Register* each morning instead of Cecelia, Kentucky. Too
many relatives have passed away since I moved
up North to marry. I should label myself Yankee, buy a plot
in Beaverdale across from my office. My father's
scythes and mauls have been picked over; the tool shed, part plank

and part log chinking, has already begun to sink. Still, I think about
our hogs as I wheel down aisles of Ferraro's Grocery
on my quest for the Christmas ham. Stacked pigs' ears, sealed
in plastic bags and ten cents per pound cheaper
if bought in bulk or feet split down the middle and crossed like

hands of the dead don't tempt me. Pork tails at $.49 a pound are too
much of a bargain to pass up. No salted crust, shrink
wrap keeps swarms of flies, mounted like polished emeralds, off
the rind. Connecticut law requires unwrapped meat to
be hung behind walls. Doors are pushed open when I ring a buzzer

but then they swing shut. Is the butcher I invent testing a blade?
Cutting is done in a hidden room and I picture walls
inflating into red balloons. Leaning to hear slaughter pen bawling,
laughter filters through. I parrot words about women
who can live for years without meat. Pulling me off my pedestal,

Aunt Hazel urges, *Buy what oozes under the plastic.* There must
be blood somewhere. Look in corners, on counters where
it might have thickened. I want a shudder that goes all the way
down my neck but orange prices plaster windows,
block my view, quench the vision of the hog, wild then stilled.

White Chickens

The image of a strait jacket has come back to me. Flat,
folded together, sleeves open and reach out like white
wings flapping the backyard my father fenced trying
to recreate the farm, chickens that ran, roosted
in a barn and laid eggs in hay. Crowded after hatching
because they were bred for slaughter, our fryers never
walked but each morning before his coffee, my father
positioned them, statues on the grass of one rooster
and ten hens that had been cooped up too long. It should
have been easy for him to wring the heads off their necks.
Was it boyhood need for chase that left him unable to kill
or did my father expect our chickens to be resurrected,
rush around the yard, plastering grass with their blood?

A Keeper

If it's warm and windless on Long Island Sound, if the tide
turns late in the morning, if high clouds block the sun,
we'll leave Longshore Boat Basin in Westport and head

across the flats inside of Seymour's Rock. We'll catch
the best of the rip on the backside of Cockenoe. Past
the tip of Saugatuck Shores, there will be a swirl,

a gull swooping to pick at bait and that will be our signal
to swing close, cut the engine and drift. First, we'll try
a Fiord spoon next to the grass, alternate pulling

and dragging as we reel in. If we get a hit, a surging run,
we may not have a bluefish. If as we work it to the side,
we see bronze stripes gleaming, we'll know it's a bass.

If it measures thirty four inches or more, we'll have
a keeper. Then we can settle back, drink a Samuel Adams
while I tell you how my father used a croppie killer

and rooster tail for lures. In Carr Creek, Kentucky,
he was baptized with a napkin tied over his hair
which the preacher blessed during the minute of total

emersion. For the rest of his life, my father used
that headrag to wipe his lures for luck so God would
be with him. He swore on the family Bible that he once

caught a gar so big that when it took off running,
the bottom burst right out of the boat. If we haven't run
out of tide before we've run out of beer, we'll head

around for Cockenoe's southwest corner, passing clumps
of reeds midway across the west side. Maybe there will be
a fly-rodder or two standing in an aluminum boat. Maybe

blackfish will swirl just as we reach the tide rip. The drift
might carry us out across the rip, around the backside
of the island. We could try a popper on a spinning rod

if our arms have not had enough, if we have more than
stories about the thirty three inch blue or the thirty two
inch striper we threw back. We need more than just

our arms spread apart estimating the size to take back
for our daughters so we can make sense of how
we spent the day. We need more than faith, we need

a blue we can fillet on the kitchen counter, one we can
hold like my father twisting the headrag in his hands,
a keeper that we can mount to hang above the fireplace.

Praying You Are Asleep

Armed with a pen to write down a recipe in case
you're not, I slide down the hall of Pinewood Manor
chanting to myself: pretend to need ingredients, ask
if it was pecans or walnuts she used for jam cake icing.

Always moving, Grandma, now you're pasted on the bed
like your wallpaper with flowers fading into red blotches.
One hundred years in disappearing, skin rises in dry ridges
and your bones are getting easier to see. It's flannel that keeps

sunlight from shining right through you. Masking pooled
urine, the antiseptic odor of old age sits between us. Go back!
Fry chicken, slice ham and green cabbage for slaw. Never
thinking like Uncle Lanny of so many crops to a field,

your vegetable garden was ploughed inward, edge
to center with furrows squaring off even while the earth
changed color under Snip and Nellie's feet. Hop
then stoop you told me. Plant cucumbers, yellow squash

next to tomatoes and peppers; save the corn for last;
keep leftover seeds sorted out in the cracked mason jars.
Hoping you will die soon, I shrink from your bedside
like I did from the scarecrow you hung on broom handles.

I don't want to finger you, smell you or hear you talk about
being a girl and riding to Oklahoma then back again to
Kentucky in covered wagons. Winding a procession of plains,
crossing over the Tennessee border, you sat right up on

the edge of the board seat, straining to see Howe Valley.
Even then you listened for a voice saying, *You have found
the promised land.* There was no sound to guide you.
Grandma, I have no words and no map to give you now.

How Sweet the Sound

Doric columns fed me into a varnished pew
where I stewed, wetter than a sheet before
it's wrung through rollers. Sin balanced scales
with wretches that were about to be food
for the gaping, flaming, wide mouth of hell.

A hog bladder blown up to bust at killing frost,
I wept at what I thought was sin: masturbation over
National Geographic. Squared off elbow to elbow,
I gave testimony to my personal savior each July
during revival at the First Methodist Church.

Lifting my chin, to show my aunts and girl cousins
that I didn't need the hymnal, I'd float through
Amazing Grace, coming closer and closer to heaven
while the preacher, a salesman during the week
at Clarks' hardware, sweated through *I was lost
but now I'm found, was blind but now I see.*

Getting the title role every Easter in the pageant —
Mary in the trailing blue bathrobe — I acted more
like our golden retriever nosing a leadstruck bird
than the mother of a dead son. Shedding feed sack
flowered print I went off to college, sat cross legged
reading poems about death that used metaphors
like sleep with no dreams, a party with no guests.

I came home to my grandmother's bedside to watch
her die with eyes looking up. No hand reached out
from the clouds pictured over the communion table.
At her service, I couldn't close the lid and smother

the crisp pink dress that she had saved for that day.
I couldn't carry the red roses draped in gold paper
letters as the casket was wheeled down the aisle.
My father, shirtsleeves rolled, held my hand while
we climbed to her grave, gaping like an open door.

With a Hand on the Limb

> *one eye glued to the tin door and one to the skylight*
> C. K. WILLIAMS

Start with A for alligator. B, C and D will blossom and ripen.
    At five, a child not ready to read alone, Todd fingers each
        shape. Until he no longer needs me to translate, I

could tell him anything; for no good reason, I might say that Q is
    R and M could be W if only he would walk on his hands
        or hold his book upside down. In his first

flourishing of interest, I overdo it, explaining what it was like
    for me as a girl growing up on a farm outside Somerset,
        Kentucky. I wrote letters up and down my fingers or

my palms with chokeberry ink, used the sweaty sides of a plow
    horse for a blackboard and hunks of clay for chalk. Walnut
        leaves helped me erase so I could start over when

I made a mistake. Bored, Todd squirms and then tilts his head as I
    flash cards. Perspective shifts: Z is N and N is Z. He asks
        if Z with lines straight across is better than N with

height and depth. Falls hurt less on the ground but he won't stay
    there forever and so we experiment. If his back
        is horizontal and his feet are vertical, he can't monkey

up our tree, swing out on a branch to throw down apples we can eat,
    letting the juice run down our chin so we can wipe our
        mouths on our sleeves. Full, we could dry the bruised

fruit for winter pies like my mother did. Slivers browned into leather
    on the silvery tin of the shed that kept in the smell of corn
        my father stored there to treat the horses when it

was cold. Take a chance, I tell Todd. Climb the tree. We'll play
catch, challenge each other to a duel of peeling. Who can
make the longest tissue thin curls, core out seeds

into slivers of half moons? As we compete, I could tell him how
the tin roof drummed out marches with the rain, slow
steady like a funeral march and how the snow

came to cover it in a quiet as peaceful as death can be for one who
believes. When my son spreads out into the light
as if he could ascend into air by staying still,

I picture Giotto's *Lamentation of Christ*, how a flock of angels
float in blue sky. Wings keep them in flight but arms
are yearning to touch earth, to cradle the body

directly below them as the mother does, her son in her lap,
both hands encircling his shoulders. Another woman
is holding his fingers, another lifts his feet

as if to inspect the puncture wounds. I can quote Dante's words
about Giotto from the *Purgatorio* but we have to reach
the last letter of the alphabet before I can come

up with an answer for the question my son has asked: picture all
the water in the world and then the smile on Noah's face
when he sees the zebras. That's how heaven will be.

No Creel Limit

The wind must have forgotten. It's August.
   There's that Long Island chop;
      fish are everywhere. Snappers are

in, roiling scalloped waves as shiners leap
   into silver fireworks, cascading
      onto the shore. Whip the boat

to full throttle! No putt, putt or hanging
   over the stern to drift, casting in
      Vermont ponds black with pines.

We want wake, spreading to angel wings.
   There must be sound, splashing,
      slapping, more than a line arcing,

more than the hiss of a swan. Don't relive
   last week with no wind to shunt
      away humidity, dilute mugginess

or ruffle the skin. This spot is guaranteed,
   no need to throw in bait shining
      like dimes in St. Barnabas' collection

plate. Solid as words filling page after page,
   the blues will hook themselves
      and jump right up into our boat

if we don't catch them. We may have been
   searching for answers, for fish
      that were not around, but today

they are on the surface, floating almost into air
   for gulls to snatch without calling,
      without diving, without getting wet.

Our Museum Selves

for Marcia Harris

Speaking of Constable, his proportion of landscape
to seascape and why it was he began to paint
in bigger canvases after marriage, we paused
so I could park your wheelchair next to a marble bench
and sit down. I'd refused to rest in Penn Station when steps,

then more steps lurking, looming, startled me like the voice
of someone I didn't think was in the room. It was as if we
stepped from the train into another life. Frightened, you gripped
your purse like an embroidered shield, becoming more and more
demanding. You made me remember wanting to slap my son,

slam him into his crib when he cried into my sleep. Even if I did,
I wouldn't admit it to you. Pulling you up to the Met when there
was no choice but to look at what we would have to descend,
I could see the approval, my elevation to sainthood in the quiet
contact with other eyes, the slight upward turn of closed lips,

the nods. I wanted to leap the steps two at a time, push your chair
handles down hard and let you roll, tightly strapped in for the ride.
Instead, I persevered, bump by bump until we passed the lions
where you played the tease, saying I ought to fall down on
my knees and give thanks that you weren't very heavy. Unable

to find another word for mule, I told you how you resembled
your brother Ed. I wish I had said it was not just love for him that
kept my right hand resting by your shoulders so you didn't need
to twist your head to be sure I was there. We moved to Gauguin
because he was on the same level and one large oil reminded us

of your father standing with five friends, three piggy backing
the other three with arms doubled around, fists clutching ties.

The photograph still sits on our piano in front of your painting :
the black and white unsettled to purple, more purple darkening
to bruise two faces, army fatigue green on another. A camera lens

was indifferent but your brush strokes were not; your hand,
though angry, was sure. Five sets of features just starting
to tip back kept insides from spilling out but not the faces
from melting as if caught in a strong wind or held under plastic
spreading over your canvas. Even after you couldn't grasp

pastel pencils, you controlled what you could, understanding
the signal like pulling on a balloon that a line holding you
had been erased. Crying that with you dead he was an only child,
Ed stood outside the door, interrupting my poetry workshop
to tell me the cause was not multiple sclerosis but the starvation

that you willed. Your brother had reached for you, straining
his forearms to give back legs, fingers strong enough to mix oils
but his hands passed through air. When your two sons wouldn't
take the ashes to scatter, we stopped the cremation. There was
nothing else we could do but bury you back in St. Louis between

your father and your mother even though we knew what you would
say, even though you couldn't run out and sit in the car to escape
their rising voices. Until he threw the first dirt while I held his
arm steady, Ed stayed nervous, anxious that during the washing,
one woman would interrupt the ritual to deny you burial because

of the green and black spider the size of a half dollar tattooed right
above where your left hip bone protruded. Marcia, at your death,
during your life, the spider wove no web, trapped nothing we
could suck juice from to dilute the bitter taste we cannot swallow
or spit on the ground. It is floating, floating still in our mouths.

Carolyn Forche's in El Salvador

but I'm next in line at the Dixwell Stop and Shop.
Artichokes, strawberries, asparagus, turkey
for economy, I figure up the total and count bills
to speed up my check out but the woman in front
of me sorts out coins. I'm impatient even though
I can see she's old with a hole in her sweater
big enough for me to stuff my fist through.
Leave enough for bus fare, the checkout clerk
urges. Her light bulbs are left behind. I buy the carton
knowing it's like dropping money in the collection
plate at church but I feel good as the bagger gives me
an approving look. I rush from the store just as
she boards the bus, bringing no light, bridging no gulf.

Christine, at Night, I Tired; Early Morning, I . . .

Late January, words spoken hastily outside my classroom
    created no clear picture like workshop poems threaded
by your mother's suicide. To compare their techniques,
    I assigned Plath and Sexton. Not satisfied, you asked
why Virginia Woolf weighted her pockets with stones,

concluding it was impossible to say just which one caused her
    her to sink. You quit coming to campus, I didn't call; dead
all these months, I didn't know. I gathered your work to publish
    a chapbook, your anguish before me like chain and mace
in a museum. Boasting about how I would address your death

with a word of life, I wrote a preface saying how short sighted
    it was to die so close to spring, that we could have built
a bonfire and as we tasted it, the scent of hickory smoke, though
    sharp, would still be alive on our tongues. No Liberty Bell
circling Long Island Sound, I kept no schedule, folded and boxed

your manuscript just as I had the scotch plaid coat I was going to
    put in a dumpster for Goodwill. Your poems were thrown
out by the painters moving my desk. Another vow I couldn't honor,
    my promise to keep your name alive was hollow, the drum
I beat on to parade my concern for the work of my students. January

sky, coral as a high collared dress you last wore or flashes of china
    black hair, startle me like a face in a picture I didn't know
had been taken. Nobody experiences anything through words: say
    Hiroshima; Kyushu's port, Nagasaki. The words atomic
bomb or nuclear shadow mean nothing to a mother nursing her son

while she ignores warnings about warring white blood cells in milk.
    The mind adjusts to anything, Christine, just as your pupils
contracted inside the closet where you hung among jackets, above

        shoes. Was the vacuum kicked aside like woman flinging
bras in Filene's Basement or were you trying to pray, a mantis with

legs slowly lifting? If I could reverse years, edit them into a film
        of a truck driver who swerves in time, your wrists turning
for me would be razored, I would call you aside. Night mushrooms
            into a cloud. What do I know about it or your mind, Christine,
thick with layers you couldn't peel away like strips of burned skin.

Monroe: Sweetheart of the Month

Right at the start, you might say
the body was what the hands were after.
Curious that something is perfectly
made, outrageous really in its
regularity: breasts, waist, thighs,
calves, ankles. Set by the camera,
weight will not mock this centerfold
from December, 1953 — *Playboy*'s
first issue was undated to ride
the newsstands as long as possible.

Posing wasn't just a matter of changing
feet. There had to be no more chilling
rarity. Clothing removed, not even a wig,
refusing to wear anything that was not
her own, she warmed both hands between
her legs as the photographer begged,
Marilyn, baby, act surprised, act ashamed.
Pinching the back of her neck to stay awake,
she thought of hot cloths for her mouth.

Seventy thousand copies sold to arms lifted
as if in blessing then lowered to smooth out
the creases again and again on her picture,
a communion wafer to be consumed or worn
like a saint's medallion on a belt buckle.
Not knowing how to get by on what
came along — Clark Gable saying *She made
a man proud to be a man* in *The Misfits*,
her last film — she thought of black
under the photographer's cloak or being
covered by sheets she had not explored.

Star

Holding two six packs of Schlitz, the man next to me
      in line at Kroger's is laughing up a storm
as his wife holds the newspaper pointing first at me, then
      my picture which is right above headlines
of a story about a woman arrested for soliciting in mid-town
      Manhattan. I'd never been to New York City
but I grabbed the *Star* knocking over a box of Life Savers
      and stacks of Mr. Goodbars. Associated Press
headlines above my picture blared: *Imposter Wears Crown;*
      Homecoming Queen Sobs! Imagine how
I felt. There wasn't a line about me in the *National Enquirer.*

Newspaper clippings from every single state in the union
      were carefully trimmed and mounted to fill
a scrapbook. I even saved the letter from an eighty year old
      man out in Oklahoma who wanted to come all
the way to Kentucky and save me. Naturally, he figured only
      a fallen woman could have such a thing happen
to her right in the middle of 50,000 people. I sure hadn't done
      anything to deserve what didn't take place
that October afternoon, but I resolved to sin as fast as possible
      in the future. I stopped attending worship
at Methodist Youth Fellowship, began writing poems filled

with desire for revenge. No more nice girl, I wouldn't give back
      my rhinestone crown to the Kitten Club, sponsors
of the event. Winning that contest had been serious business;
      my Kappa Delta sisters must have hung at least
two hundred posters around UK's campus and believe me, it
      was no picnic finding a suit in just the right blue.
Our pledges handed out leaflets in the CU at noon, tied balloons
      stenciled with *Victory for Vivian* on car antennas

and passed out Dum-Dum's in the library while wearing
    tee-shirts that said, *We're Suckers for Shipley*.
My rival struck back, plastering flyers over all of the campus

windows saying, *Shipley Sucks*. I for one wouldn't stoop to
    dirty tactics but I did try to get her arrested for
defacing state property. My campaign manager hadn't counted
    on Cotton Nash's girlfriend getting elected to
Homecoming Court. At the University of Kentucky, basketball
    brought in big money and Adolph Rupp liked to
keep his star players happy. Julie was crowned; I cried; Cotton
    beamed and my escort shouted, *You've crowned
the wrong girl!* Open the album. It's over on the piano. Trophy
    clutched, roses hanging at my side like a hand
broken from its wrist, the first picture of me is with my mouth

twisted. I was standing on the fifty yard line just off the field.
    It was right after the half time show when
President Oswald himself came to correct the gross injustice.
    I tinted that photo from the *Star* and enlarged
my face. As paint aged, it became opaque. Original lines haunt
    the portrait like a specter: 1960's hair, blooming;
eyes and my smile fixed as if hooked at the breastbone. Thirty
    years later, I can say anything. For example,
I might go to a therapist who would help me recall seeing the AD
    switch the names so the announcer would crown
the wrong girl. Maybe that happened, maybe it didn't, but Rupp's

innocence can't be proved. He's dead and there wasn't a chapter
    about me in his biography. The orders could
have been given by University Public Relations to attract press
    to Lexington. I might unearth Senator McCarthy,
get him to start an investigation, have the FBI find if there was
    a plot to undermine democracy by ignoring student
votes, the voice of the American people. I suppose it's possible
    that the Communists had infiltrated the election,
figuring they'd practice first on a Homecoming Queen, then move

>	on to the White House. Not letting go of that Saturday
afternoon is as productive as speculating on afterlife. If I stepped

back onto that field, I guess I'd still be whimpering to reporters,
>	*I feel like a clod!* or agreeing with the Student
Council's leader that the word *queen* must have been misplaced
>	like an unframed photograph, never questioning
why the runner-up was given my crown. Anyway, I would have
>	run even if I'd known the consequences. It
would have been a shame to miss all of those headlines. Now, I
>	want to turn, go up to myself at twenty and shout:
Grab the roses, flash the bird! Sprint the stadium. Rip out kleenex
>	you stuffed in your bra, shred Marilyn's breasts,
fling them on the turf like a wildcat to confetti your own parade.

Outside the Rainbow

Phillis Wheatley, kidnapped at seven or eight
from childhood of ebony, jet, onyx,
you wore a velvet dress three times
to mourn giving birth to infants
who would curl into bats.
Chokecherries, panthers
you dreamed, sooty boards
you scrubbed, tar you feared,
John Peters' fists you felt. No voodoo
but magic printed on the page: *To S.M.*
a Young African Painter, on Seeing His Works.

Moonshine

Walking back from services in the sweat of evening, my mother
and I stopped to be civil. Just by sitting, Uncle Alvey possessed
his porch, his dog. I felt cork in his leg, an old war wound, making
sure my birth paid for the *pain of woman* mother used as a whip
to make me behave. Past the age to admit my fingers tightened

her glove, I stood while mother told everyone that I was bound
for Lexington that next fall. Our preacher had warned me
of strong drink, shouting: a train, a beerbelly, hands puzzling over
the body. I had already learned from cousins to pay him no mind.
Deciding to tie one on, I found barrels and copper sheeting

out by the corner shed. Drinking from a still with condensers
made of automobile radiators that left lead salts was as deadly
as selling to strangers. I had heard Uncle Lanny's prohibition
stories about his neighbors who had drawn big claims, sometimes
as much as thirty dollars, to witness against a friend. Hard times,

everybody needed money. Government set people against each other.
Trusting my father to have sense enough not to use soldered joints,
that I would not be blinded, I drank. Climbing onto a man's world,
Jack, flinging red and yellow beans, I got higher and higher, putting
miles between me and women rocking, smothering in oilcloth.

Another drink, one more and I was sitting with the men on a bench
inside Alexander's grocery: crock, bare floors, charred coffeepot
and skillet set on a wood stove. Eating buttermilk biscuit, sorghum,
fried ham from fingers still holding the smell of livestock, there
was enough for feasting but nothing left over to clean up, store

in the press for breakfast. No ceremony, no grace, a sleeve to wipe
gravy with and one plate to clean, there were no women to hide me

from men, from the real life lived out of doors. No Kentucky sounds, it's Connecticut rain dropping like thirty years that have run together. Leaning right up against the bar at Rudy's, I don't have to hide behind

lattice work around the back porch as I drink Henry McKenna. Marty fills my glass: a shot; a beer; a shot; a beer. Another round and I lift white lightning in the dipper. Tin freckled with rust drains away to frayed hooked rugs, Clabber Girl barns, beans rattling on strings, chicken heads dripping, the scraps from my grandmother that I stitch into a crazy quilt.

Here's Looking at You, Kid

Heavy, ears stick out, teeth gone: the Village, New York,
you tell me, your jaw split by a lover. Crossing America,
you stretched out on garage floors to keep your woman,
her kidneys off the cement. Never did you dream your dream
of childhood, your mother not in it. At the bar, forearms,
ferns drape; you rise trying to imitate Humphrey Bogart.
We're not at Rick's place in Casablanca but Archie Moore's
in New Haven. Ingrid Bergman's legs are not entwined
with the stool. You wouldn't worry about driving to Norwich
if you could be sure when you step out the side exit
that Claude would be there shouting to Humphrey, *Round up
the usual suspects in the morning.* No such ending for you, no
airplane, just seven flights of factory stairs to sweep to earn rent.
It's early afternoon. Give me your Maine childhood again. Dream
your dream of childhood. Put your mother in it. Let's keep buying
rounds of Elm City until we stop worrying about the time and
forget that we'll never wake up young like their faces on a screen.

Hitchhiking Mass. Pike

Don't ask! I'm not a chairman or dean.
I can't give you my class to pad
the silence, old age. You are you. No
ash tree that burns returning again
to bloom but Custer blue spruce,
dying one branch at a time. Only
the top is left and with no new growth,
stubs mount in rings like the years,
broken. Your trunk refuses to snap
as legs of our bar stool might do.

We're in doubt. What's real? Perhaps
what the orthopedist calls spine
is looking glass. Proof is in touch.
If the mirror should slip an inch,
two, we'd have one eye or Van Gogh's ear.
A foot or more, a shoulder's gone —
nothing to rub. Further, no hands
to clasp bottles of Jack Daniels
doubled by the wall. Uncertainty
is exhilarating like that fall Sunday
after our reading at Stone Soup
of will we or won't we. Your coat
dragging like a matador's cape
as we flagged cars, worrying
about the time as if we could
negotiate anything. No ride.
Your thumb stayed, stuck out
like your fears, like your dreams.

Week Four: Story About Another Person

Drink to the bird
E. A. ROBINSON

Pad in hand, I decide to do research, get a first person account
for the next assignment. A prize in *Folio*, publication by *Intro*

don't interest me but getting an *A* in fiction writing does.
Winter hardens New Haven; wind that chips sleeves and

pockets makes the men who piss behind stairways on Lake Place,
crooning syllables to muscatel, sad to have hands, spiderbones.

Five years ago, Tony had just enough to rent a private room
at the Taft. Spring days, he could lean on the sill in a sleeveless

undershirt and put his head out of the window. Now he's lucky
if he can sleep at Viva Zapata on rice bags the cooks store in piles

near the furnace to keep them dry. Most days, Tony takes up
a barstool at Rudy's on the corner of Elm and Howe. Marty

the bartender lets him use the john with just enough light to read
handwriting of some twenty year old who doesn't care enough

to dot the *I* or cross the *T*. A tall blond girl from Yale drinks
supported by Whaler's banners, Raven's baseballs, football

photos taken at the Bowl. To show her what I know, just how
clever I can be, I quote *Drink? or think? better drink.* Now

that Bukowski's dead, there's a spot I can fill. I don't need
to live his life to get the lines he wrote. Since I'm a regular

from the state school across town, I pick up Tony's tab for
Jack Daniels and Sam Adams, and say I'm from *Southern News* to

buy the right for an interview I'll use in a story: *Tony, what
makes you drink shots and beer at nine o'clock in the morning?*

Tactful, I make mental notes, he mumbles about Champion Auto,
how he operated two bays at one time, two bays at one time.

For the price of another round, I can gather authentic detail, get
Tony to talk about how he ended World War II by slicing wrists

but bleeding was too slow. Each drink brings him closer to the bar,
face fallen forward. Some days he cuts his forehead on the edge

but the bouncer lets him sit and drink as long as he's good for
business at Rudy's. The owner has left orders about what to do

if Tony starts to shake his fist and mutter to no one in particular,
You goddamn Yalie, I operated two bays at one time, two at one time.

We Were Wrong, Terribly Wrong

ROBERT S. McNAMARA,
Secretary of Defense, 1961-1968

Dressed in a black three piece suit with a roll of toilet paper
    in one hand and a Bible in the other, your brother starts
at the corner of Wooster Square Park on Chapel Street
    then parades until he spots an elm that suits him. Before

spending two years in Vietnam, he would walk up State Street
    to the front window of Denton's Drug Store and stand
looking at Joseph Rosenthal's AP photograph of an American flag
    being raised on Mt. Suribachi at the top of Iwo Jima.

In WWII, when the Fifth Marine Division made it to the summit
    after four days of battle, your father was one of six men
who raised the flag. He died within days. It was late February,
    early March of 1945. There were little banners in almost all

windows with stars on them. Blue meant someone from that house
    was in the service and a gold star meant someone had died.
Your grandmother's house had three stars, two blue, one gold.
    Then two turned to gold. Your brother still has the letters

written by your father about the firefights: Marines would hold up
    their weapons over a ridge, exposing only hands and upper arms
to return fire. Those letters were filled with Ira Hayes, a Pima Indian
    who also raised the flag but who survived to die of alcohol.

Hayes would pop up to fire, flop back down to reload. During
    one mortar attack, he walked off to relieve himself.
Six thousand, two hundred died on Iwo Jima in shallow gulches,
    from snipers, shells being lobbed. Hayes was the soldier

your brother wanted to be when he enlisted and asked to be
        shipped to Da Nang. There were no flags to raise, no pictures
placed in Denton's Drugs, no stars in front windows. Not killed
        in battle like your father, your brother couldn't drown

himself in shots and beers like Hayes. He would take nothing
        from the living but couldn't stop what the dead took from
him. Shouting at the elm tree he's picked about bodies splitting
        the surface, your brother hurls the roll of paper high into air.

Is each layer a beginning , wiping out years in Vietnam that are
        like ice on the window spreading into a jungle of ferns
or waiting fingers? Streaming like a rocket unrolling all the way
        to heaven, the tissue always misses the branches and piles

in the street. Shrugging it off, your brother goes back home
        to your mother who never complains about the mess
but worries over the extravagance of it, the waste of good paper.
        Your cousin Joyce stuffed cotton in her cheeks to fill them out

but she didn't throw it away. Dried over night, cotton could be
        used again and again. The toilet paper is useless, melting
into the street like the years your brother spent waiting out dark
        knowing every stumbling place his hand might touch down

on a face. The eyes were always open, darker than veined coca
        leaves or concentrated pools of light like silk from Hanoi.
Sucked back again, your brother confronts the eyes, your father, and,
        the look in his eyes as he braces to raise the flag, making

shoulders ache with the permanence of it. No Rosenthal
        photograph of your brother in Denton's Drugs, no red, white
and blue only black, lined into a wall of eyes that will never close,
        that will never disappear, that words of remorse cannot erase.

Don't Buy *The New Haven Register*

Catch the week on Saturday, again Sunday when you scrub
white marble of the Beinecke Library, its walls a shield
for William Blake's *Songs of Innocence and Experience*

with the tyger and lamb you'll never get time off to see.
They ought to erect a monument to you, a bronze statue
by Johnson of a man squatting in a red Giant's cap,

blue glitter worn down. Scouring the latest insurrection
with Top Job and full strength ammonia, there's only time
for two cigarettes before and after punching the clock.

11,000 slabs are perfect canvas for a night priest, aerosol
in hand stenciling the week's massacre. Always popular
is the P.L.O. or Israel. Lately, it's been S's you erase :

Serbs, Somalia, El Salvador. You wonder if like a Yale
professor making up a final exam, you could leave *Viva*
and let artists fill in the blank. But you're paid by the hour

to clean, so why should you care? Keep workdays clean;
bless the politicians; bless the spray painters. If letters
don't drip down this marble, you'll have black top to clean

since revolutions resurface bubbling through asphalt cracks.
James Jones might have watched you walking every day past
Naples Pizza and dreamed up the title *From Here to Eternity*.

No Burt Lancaster, you'll never make love with waves
crashing around you and Deborah Kerr. No WWII beach.
No passion. Just reds, oranges, yellows, blues and black.

How to Find George Sterling: Revise the Canon

Or, stand on a street corner in the Tenderloin. The search
begins with an embrace. A swift ballet, your wallet
is gone. The round trip ticket from San Francisco is still

in your hotel room with a flight number, departure date
and time. This is a break. Don't call American Express!
Move to a different hotel. You can buy a blue tweed jacket

at the Salvation Army in the Outer Mission. Throw it over
your left shoulder like George Sterling did on Sixteenth
Street. You can go underground forever, become invisible

for a few hours or for a few days. It was a lucky break
your wallet was lifted. Otherwise, to achieve this sensation,
you'd have to give twenties, fifties then hundred dollar bills

to more and more men warming the street before you could
go deeper into the Mission to bargain for a *carne asada*
burrito at the Roosevelt Tamale Parlor or buy a hex cooped

up in either ointment, a candle or aerosol. At first, you
should do nothing more daring than go to the Castro and sip
an expresso at the Cafe Flore. Build up to working the spell

you bought into a triple: slide into North Beach and steal
back the twentieth century, evaporate from a Barbary Coast
saloon, solidify in an opium den. You'll find George Sterling

seated sharing a water pipe with Robinson Jeffers. Be sure
to save enough magic to get back home so you can hike up
Telegraph Hill, walking on wooden boards to the shanties

that brought Kerouac pure joy. Push straight on through
commuters waiting for the bus by a red striped curb right

under the big gold letters of City Lights Bookstore. Its

doors shoulder plate glass that protects pyramids of *Howl*
and *On the Road*. Edge down to the basement, plug a tape
in you smuggled all the way back from the Barbary Coast:

George Sterling reciting *Lilith* and *Testimony of the Suns*.
Inhale absinthe or drink the medoc stuffed behind the dark
narrow shelves and let the fog outside digest you. Then go

deeper, deeper where the census taker never polls. Ducks
ribbon King Tin Restaurant; resist them. Avert your eyes
from the ichthyosaurs on crushed ice. To find Sterling, you

must go further, even further to the last room fragrant with
perilla, rape seed, sesame and mustard. Open the thirteenth
drawer of the acupuncturist Sterling consulted for old pain;

see what is desiccated. When he was here, the signage was
all different, the streets, the restaurant aisles much too close.
There was no one to wire money from home. Don't give up.

No longer a tourist, you can't bend your knees and hope
for an earthquake. To find him, you must secret yourself
on top of Russian Hill. Pose as a flower poking through

the laurel leaves that filter cruise ships going from the bay
into the Pacific. When it is exactly one half hour before
sunset, while there is still time to see, go to the end of

a path. You will know the one; it is overgrown. What you
will find is rather small, a stone cut in the only words of
George Sterling left in San Francisco that you can finger:

*Tho' the dark be cold and blind, Yet the sea fog's touch
is kind, And her mightier caress Is Joy and the pain
thereof; And great is thy tenderness, cool gray city of love.*

Why I Fish

> *Nor need you mind the serial ordeal*
> ROBERT FROST

1. I fish when three sons and a husband are not enough.

A fan unfolding, water bands the cove signaling the first sign
of spring in Long Island Sound: winter flounder. The key
word to learn is chum, a mixture of clams, mussels, and fish
parts allowed to thaw in a bag and let drift in the current.
The manual reads drop a sandworm and you'll see flounder.
That's not worked for me but I've scored with bucktails, Redfin
or Bomber by Connecticut River's mouth and Watch Hill.

2. I fish because I don't want summer to end.

Chum can be abandoned since summer flounder called fluke
like a clean sandy bottom. Bigger than winter flounder, they
have teeth, feed on small fish but will hit a variety of bait. I've
caught fluke in the red-hot Norwalk Islands on live snappers,
herring or squid strips. Reciting verse helps to fill dry spells:
*And if you're lost enough to find yourself /By now, pull in
your ladder road behind you/And put a sign up CLOSED.*

3. I fish to find what's missing: friends to call I don't have.

Poetry won't wilt the memory: me, standing behind the podium
after the fiction reading, counting the money collected for *Folio*
as everyone else has gone out to drink at the Cape Codder.
Driving home, I invent reasons I wasn't asked: I didn't know Felix
the Cat was acid; I didn't have a sun tattooed on my forearm; I was
too fat, too old, too much the mother. I tried to wash off loneliness
all the next day but it stayed like a wine stain that wouldn't soak out.

4. I fish since searches never end: looking for keys, love, flounder.

I have learned how to forget. Like an atom, I have sought company
of others, tired of carrying the whole weight of memory like
an audience: parents, brothers, sisters, lovers. Surely, heaven will
be stripped of need for talk, for touch, for hope. Even when I know
summer is gone, that fish on Morgan Point's bottom have migrated
to deep water off shore, I fish, keeping lures that worked before,
letting chum drift for the flounder I can't see that might be there.

Am Braighe

I

Gibberish I called it but in Gaelic, you scolded, it was
higher ground sought by your people from the hillside Braes
or the Lochaber district of the Highlands. We found *Am Braighe*
below the Cabot Strait on Nova Scotia's hills that brooded,

by lakes misted over like those in Scotland during the 1840's
when your great-grandfather left, cleaned like rocks from his farm
by a landlord who earned more money shearing herds of sheep
than collecting the rent. Gaelic Language, Celtic soul, you swear

you heard the *am fidhlear* in your mother's womb. Translating
to fiddle for me, you kept time with fall tunes, stomping dancers
and tall tales: walking herrings, fair-haired priests who looked to
the sky so much they got stuck in it. Watching the Rankin Family

fiddle — their staccato bowing got them four trophies in March at
the Juno awards — we danced to *Cregnish Hills, Miss Lyall's Reel*,
sang right along with *Mason's Apron* and *High Road to Linton*.
Your earrings dripped into gold and swayed in the rising applause.

II

It was early afternoon but your father was already asleep when
we came to say goodbye, when you came to say I *love you* to him,
the words I had rehearsed with you, struggling to pull them out
with each step we took up the Cape Breton hill to his house.

Baddeck was below us and Big Harbour. Moored in the bay, you
could not say the three words for me. Your father would not say
them to you but you leaned over him needing to hear what
your father would not say, what he would never say: *Come back*.

There were the words he did not phone or send you on the day
your mother died. As if asleep, the cancer was behind her eyes,

hidden like the penny in birthday cakes she iced for you before she
sent you away to school. I couldn't give you last words from her.

III

The details of my own brain tumor dissolved your sadness and
the space that had settled around us but now there is silence when
I want to talk to you. Speak. All or nothing, Wendy, but not this. It
was crazy when you were here, falling asleep in mid-afternoon,

waking only when my sons came home from soccer practice for egg
rolls and special lo-mein without peapods. Where did words you
would not say go? Do the words we did not say stay? Each night,
I stop myself from going to stand at a gate in New Haven Terminal

to hear the train I dream you on. A ticket agent poses, one boot
on the counter as if his other is too heavy to lift. I listen for your
voice to whisper what you have not said. A train arrives, people
crowd by but you do not. Soon, the blackboard schedule is erased.

Action News, Channel Eight

It's not the woman crying, her dead son, the unfenced
   tracks or the train and driver that we talk
      about. It's the camera, the photographer who keeps

filming, zooming in for a close up of the mouth while
   a policeman holds her back right
      when she learns who is dead. Clouds pack the sky,

a blue heron slips while spearing a fish and we laugh,
   letting our *New Yorkers* drop. Still, last
      night's six o'clock news, the tightened lips intrude.

In a day or two, when we pause, we probably won't think
   of that mouth, the mother in New Haven with
      no son, no morning or bacon to fry for him to smell.

Results of the Blood Test

the doctor just reeled off to me confirm what the loose skin
    around my neck has predicted: no more ovulation,
no more children. No questions, I cradle the phone, press my head
    on a window to cool down while my breath fogs
the glass blooming to a shape my body can create. Waiting in line
    at Stop and Shop, will I want to ask the mother who
might be standing behind me if I can smell her son's head, stick
    my index finger through his fist? I can feel
blacktop, being stretched out with November heat soaking my son
    as I sat reading to him about starfish with arms
called rays. No eyes, no ears, no nose, the starfish probed, poked
    and groped to fill the tiny mouth on his underside.
First, his rays would go over and under a mussel. An oyster, clam
    or snail, they all smelled the same to him.
The starfish humped then pulled, pulled then humped an available
    shell until it opened and the insides could be sucked
out. Even when you are very hungry, I can hear myself preaching
    to Todd, eat very slowly and with love, choosing
only an oyster. Lick the soft skin, tongue the hole and swallow
    juice but leave meat attached. Maybe, a pearl,
even two, might seed. A starfish could lose a ray if a crab jerked
    one off or a rock fell but another ray would grow.
Open to any attack, starfish hid under rocks in tidal pools out on
    Morgan Point where there was no sunlight, no
danger. Taking the telephone off the hook so there can be no more
    news, I smooth my son's prom picture, the one
he had taken his junior year. That was two months before night
    pavement slicked and the evergreen reached out
for Scott McNeill. To soothe his mother at the wake, I pontificated
    saying to risk remembering is better than not knowing.
To keep the lesson of Scott's death alive, I helped the high school
    establish a scholarship and raise money by printing

Bob Marley's *One Love* on a tee shirt, the one I started to dust with
    last week. Amputations do heal. When the bleeding
finally stops, I will pin over the stump to clothe it from the curious
    but I'll feel the weight that will never press or
bulge my stomach like the movement of a foot on a phantom limb.

Color

Air strikes like steel
down my lungs
        stiffens to breath
        crisp like tearing paper
                the sound of my shoes
                printing into asphalt.

A cardinal poses
brief as blood
        red on white mounds
        silkened tents
                or tissue paper breasts
                swollen and wet.

Ice clear flesh
on brittle bones
        thin as a twig on
        the fingers of trees
                planted by my sons
                who punctuate the snow
                        with black periods. My body
                        drips no color as I run here.

Our Bodies, Arms of a Weathervane Pointing North and South,

Connecticut and Virginia, we walk Appomattox, peeling years
that wallpaper our graduate school selves. Martha, we are

growing old; I would not travel except to see you. I dwell
on my face and how it must look to you now, how my waist

has thickened. Getting off the plane, I sucked in but had to sag
back into myself. We repeat names as if fingering beads:

Cliff, Bill, Jimbo, Harry, Anne and Jennalie. I want to float out
over the corpse of my body while Cliff forgets the cigarette

he holds as he dances with me. How beautiful was the saint
we wanted to pursue: Dr. Duncan who fished through coffee

money in Old Central, unsure of how many nickels he had put
in the plate. A cup, we can pass him between us like our notes

on Ruskin, Morris and Pater that we shared in his Victorian
seminar. We pause before the ice house overlooking what

might have been a point in the river where soldiers could cross
for breath in the wood. Death has cored this place like the hole

that held ice in walls of rough plank. There would have been
a pole with a hook that hung from a spike, a room where saws

were kept, a floor that always stayed damp and cool. You explain
how ice was chunked and layered with straw to last the summer

and pretend to be the cook who opened then quickly closed
the door to keep in winter. I picture us hanging up sere leaves

of lavender, lupine or indian leaf from the overhang. It's quiet
now in McLean House, the doorway flanked with hollyhocks,

the rose and yellows contrasting their brave colors like the blue
and grey. In the photograph over an oval table with a marble top,

Grant and Lee are sitting right above where they must have been
sitting on April 9, 1865, as they will sit forever posing between

the two sets of curtains, now crimson velvet that spills on the floor.
Like countless takes of Clark Gable and Vivien Leigh's farewell

that Victor Fleming ordered in 1939 directing *Gone with the Wind*,
I add then cut detail after detail from scenes that might have been

enacted on these fields. I create a starring role for myself, waking
the morning after a battle, turning to cradle the head of my brother

in my hands that are positioned the same way they were when I held
the bulb of an amaryllis I had forgotten to take indoors after giving

it a day of cold in early spring. The temperature had dipped below
freezing that night and there was no resurrecting the plant. What I

had left was memory of that one March day, the white blooming,
bending almost into the earth. Martha, we have awakened no rumble

of cannon but when the guard's not looking, we can stroke flow blue
dishes. General Lee wouldn't eat without them as if each meal was

the source that renewed his passion. The taste of dust rising stays
in our mouths. We've let our bodies go too long, let more than years

lapse. Let's resolve to go on a fat-free diet, meet next year at a spa.
I'll draw the line, however, at liposuction, doing our eyes. Laughing

at our thighs, magic between us returns and if we could only linger,
The Lady of Shalott might drift by. Nothing happens but moving

shadows across quiet water and the stirring of heavy headed iris
so bronze and so big, they might be lanterns. Almost as if we are

rehearsing our senior play, we repeat, *She has a lovely face. God
in his mercy lend her grace.* Subdued like the green by stillness,

we listen as a rising wind predicts autumn to the leaves that must
know what is forming in the trees just as the Confederates had to

suspect that Union troops were just over the rise. Now, as soldiers
must have done the last day, we listen for a voice to say, *Surrender.*

When Your Number's Up

Rocking on the front porch with eyes closed to feel late sun,
    my grandmother preached to her congregation of dogs,
cats, chickens, *The hairs of your head are numbered.*
    I pictured her hands, laced fingers reaching
to knuckles and thumbs twiddling like blades of a reel mower

cutting hay, as a barber shaved my head with an electric razor.
    Piling around me like stacks of wheat
before it is gathered and tied in Bruegel's *The Harvesters,*
    my hair was red then gold in the air
as it dropped. *Way too pretty to throw away,* the orderly

said as he gathered it in a sack for me to keep. The night
    before the meningioma was removed,
I had to translate the medical word for brain tumor to my kin
    as they circled around me. Holding
hands while they sang hymns, their trust was in the mighty

fortress of god not the surgeon. Layering my fingers into
    my palms, index fingers and thumbs
pointed to heaven, I used to play *Here's the church, here's*
    the steeple. Open the doors and here's
the people. During the operation, my hands were strapped

down and I couldn't pray without them. I lived; I could count.
    Emptying the bag I brought from Gaylord,
I laid each strand of hair on the bedspread, told myself: quick,
    number your arm, go to Lighthouse Liquors,
buy fistfuls of Quik Pic, Daily Lotto, Play Four and Power Ball.

Ice Bites Inward

White has been dropping
as long as you can remember.
Running through March snow
you feel it fall behind you.
At a certain moment, the ground
is no longer brown the way
day drifts to dark. You almost see
color go but you always look away
just as light is evaporating
like the last drop of water pooled
on asphalt. When you exhale,
there is a cloud. Will a thought
slip in, cause you to miss
the breath that separates a moment
from your last? Flakes fill this night
one by one, countless like years.
In such whiteness, ice invents itself;
never look up or back, only on.

Like a Peacock, or So Folks Said

Flowering boards with paper, sweeping, painting,
stenciling or keeping dirt out, Minnie Taber, you always

were proud, sitting in the parlor room each Sunday
to teach me how to turn the crank on the Victrola

so the records didn't skip or drag out the music. Stilled,
you show me how to live; you don't want tubes down

your nose: *Land sakes, child, what a sight I'd make!*
One hundred and one years shrink to nothing. You are

bone as I finger scars on your wrist, cut not by a razor
circling but the barbed wire you climbed trying to keep

cows in the front field. You have forgotten how much
flour and lard you used to bake biscuit; tornados that

ripped Kentucky taking a barn are too big to talk
about. Instead, we picture Hardin County and the pear

trees, white halves you still think you will get to can
in syrup so thick my spoon will float. Your house is torn

down to its ribs. Wide poplar beams are exposed again,
straight firm smooth light yellow as the day they were

first hewn and Grandpa hauled them by a horse sled
to the top of the hill where you stood that Friday before

your wedding. Mottled yellow-green linoleum rots
your kitchen floor and the Jackson Press is gone;

it was your mother's and built by her father to keep
flies off Sunday dinner. I won't tell you how my father,

your youngest child, sold it off along with the oak sewing
table he had built. Your canned sweet pickles, Clorox bottles

I cut to hold bird seed, Popsicle sticks I stacked and glued
into a napkin holder are all gone like green mason jars

emptied of peaches and bargained for by mouths that
had never tasted your pies and tried to guess, *Lard?*

An extra spoonful was your secret. Nothing's preserved
except in your memory. If you die, what will be left for me

to hold? Last Saturday, my father put everything up to auction
with paddles waving in raised hands that never knew you.

The Obituary

I'm writing for myself won't read like my mother's
grocery list. Stacked, cans of prune juice, red kidney beans

and hominy formed her monument with bars of Ivory
and Brillo scouring pads for a base. No ordinary

Kentucky limestone would do for her. Pink veined marble
was chiseled in days she spent numbered by sink, refrigerator

and stove. To flesh out the final memory of myself I plan
to leave for my three sons, to show what a rebel I really could

have been, I will mention the Dixwell Stop and Shop where
I donned a beret, scissored labels, leaving cans silvered

bullets or metal stove pipes while my mother stood near a shelf
fingering soups as if the choice of mushroom, chicken noodle

or tomato mattered to my father. In the last summary of my life,
rather than list clubs I joined, I'll include melons I have known:

Casaba, creamy white and sweet; Persian, pink-orange
and almost spicy; Cranshaw, a cross between the two;

Santa Claus, green and slightly sweet and as a grand finale,
the orange fleshed Honeydew. Never a Julia Child or Gael Greene,

I'll ask *The New Haven Register* to include my grandma's recipe
for jam cake with raisins, black walnuts, coconut, nutmeg,

cinnamon, blackberry preserves, crushed pineapple and her secret
ingredient of three teaspoons of cocoa. At last, I will even dare

to reveal in print the joy I took from each tip of very young
asparagus, teething then mouthing the stalk whole and that

I had upon more than one occasion tongued an avocado probing
yellow then the green. To top off my column, I'll paste a picture

of me, marked *Early Photo,* sitting out on the open deck in an empty
hot tub, buck naked, while I suck the hair of a mango seed dry.

An Old Husband's Tale

> *how it takes place / While someone else is eating*
> W. H. AUDEN

Daedalus was not a man, Icarus no boy. That's a myth.
Without a husband to bind her, Daedalus turned nature
inside out, taught her daughter to fly from earth; after all,

men couldn't fence air. Feathering Icarus in sequence
as a pan pipe rises, Daedalus twined quills to mold two sets
of wings sealed in an icing of white wax stiff as bridal lace.

Daedalus hovered, warning: *Keep mid-way; water weights
and sun burns. Always follow me.* Icarus rose or was pulled
up, casting her shadow on a ploughman, head lifted from

his rut, who grumbled, *A woman's place is in the home.*
The mother tried to lift her arms higher to buffer her daughter
but blue enveloped Icarus who cried, *Let's fly all the way*

to Trinacria. Knowing Samos was north and Calymne east,
Icarus ignored the earth's warning being traced out for her
by the sharded coast of Crete. Filial duty cannot blot desire

as the moon eclipses the sun. Perhaps there was a brilliance
gleaming in Icarus' green eyes that flashed, mercifully
blocking the sight for Daedalus: her only child encircling

wings writhing like a corn snake carried aloft by a hawk.
Imagine the girl, her mother's support failing, the aerial lift
and impulse spent. Dripping to the sea, only the wax

hissed, floating as islands do. Daedalus did not fly again.
Unused, feathers yellowed; wax stiffened into her wings
that stretched out more like a shroud than a swan in flight.

A Rose by Any Other Name Would Smell as Sweet

    a.
Shakespeare, you should revise, contemporize
Romeo and Juliet for the 21st century. The last name

of my son, my step-son to be precise, would be sweeter
if it didn't trumpet out another man's name, if it echoed

my own. Matthew is hammocked between us and I feel
the biological father behind me like antediluvian rock

that will not shift no matter how many soccer games
or band concerts I endure. If I shut my eyes, I might have

been the verb in his conception, the heat inside the womb,
laying claim to all that is beautiful. I am captive of a desire,

however primitive, to own my son in this modern wreck
that is our life. Matthew's mother, who learned to decode

him before there were words, does not share my need
to recognize her name on a school program. Her world

has healed. First, each day went on without a husband
as children walked to school, ran back to let themselves

in the house. If she remembered laughter, it was a dream
in which she barely smiled. Some afternoons, she might

have thought of shoulders splintering a door, then her own
moans or she might not. She never let her son know.

    b.
Stopping his questions, she could not silence voices
louder than church bells that began to cuckoo: he's not

their birth father, not their sperm father. Like a student
in Chaucer framing class notes with her professor's initials,

I wrote my son's first name with my last name again
and again. No scientist, I couldn't alter biology or erase

Enquirer headlines that daily inked a step-father who raped
then strangled a five year old by stuffing underwear down

his throat. It was always the step-father. Without her own
name, Cinderella's wicked step-mother became obsolete.

    c.
Teaching Matthew to read in second grade, I was tempted
to rewrite Webster's and erase *step* from his vocabulary.

Our favorite author was Hans Christian Andersen, so we
read *The Snow Queen* night after night. In winter, the holly

tree looked like the bush of red berries half buried in snow
where the reindeer put Gerda down. On the afternoons when

Matthew came home with another story about the whole class
laughing at him as he stumbled over words during Take a Turn

during library, I was reinforced by the constancy Gerda showed
in the glacial search for her brother Kay who had been lured

away and then enchanted by the Snow Queen. When it
was my son's turn to parade a sign advertising the book

fair, I reminded him about Gerda who didn't give up but
carried words written by the Lapland woman on a piece

of dried fish to the old Finland woman who learned
them by heart. She ate the fish in her porridge but all

Matthew needed to do was memorize the announcement
he had to carry in the halls and then pretend to read it.

    d.

Words are pronounced by rules, I'd announce while I
drummed my fingers on the counter top. We scanned line

after line lost in shapes that had nothing to do with meaning
but clotted the line with long and short vowels, accented

and unaccented beats. Turning letters as if they were pieces
in a Chinese puzzle, Matthew placed index cards around

syllables, frozen for him like the 100 pieces of ice that were
almost exactly alike surrounding Kay on the Snow Queen's

lake. The life in his hands numbed, Kay shaped out whole
sentences with ice, failing each time to fit edges together

that spelled *Eternity,* the key to undoing the Snow Queen's
spell. With his skates back on, he would be his own master.

    e.

Like an eternity for me, the alphabet elongated beyond all
meaning for Matthew. Each cipher was as precious to him

as a dictionary to tourists in another country because it
freed them from a translator and they could travel back streets

alone. Guessing at some words, it was the familiar shapes,
the recognized, that kept my son trying to read. Consonants

would clack on our tongues. The vowels though small
in number were a regiment blocking any steady progress

by constantly shifting battle formations like the snow flakes
changing patterns to attack Gerda as she struggled to find

Kay. At first, Matthew learned sounds, not combinations,
whispering in my ear so his mother wouldn't hear him

and take a shower, muffling her sorrow with water. Fingering
words he could pronounce as if hopping on rocks across

a page, when he stumbled, he would turn to me. Soon, he
mouthed a whole line of print with no stammering. If they

had been animated into cartoon characters, surely letters
would have risen up like the ice pieces that danced for joy

when Gerda's tears melted the glass splinter in Kay's heart.
Tired, ice shards fell, formed *Eternity* of their own accord.

    f.

On our first vacation after becoming a family, we drove
from Connecticut to California. Unable to read road signs,

Matthew made a game of spotting the Jerusalem Artichoke
lacing the highways of every state. Debating whether

to label the sunflowers golden, orange or yellow, the first
one of us to spot their big heads when we came to a border

got a dollar to spend at the next rest stop. From Audubon's
guide, we learned the Jerusalem Artichoke was planted by

Indians then spread eastward. In 1805, Lewis and Clark
dined on the tubers baked by a squaw in territory later

labeled North Dakota. Clark recorded Jerusalem Artichoke
with its potato like texture and sweet, nut-like taste into

a diary. The common name for the flower was a corruption
of the Italian *girasole*, meaning *turning to the sun*. Black,

the eyes were like holes in a tanned leather belt. Reminded
that what the states had in common bound them together

not the name of the country, my heart kept troping toward
my son but I was unable to stem the yearning to reseed.

On his eighth birthday, Matthew read the fortune cookies
to party guests at the China Inn. Seeing him exorcize ghosts

word by word, no tears melted glass splinters in my eye or
heart that silvered over to mirror another. I did have an answer

for Juliet's question to Romeo: *What's in a name?* On Matthew
mine would have become the jigsaw piece I used to dovetail

a ragged border like *girasole* crossing boundaries cohering
east to the west, naturally connecting one coast to another.

As If Corn Could Invent Itself

I've come back, father, though to a day I didn't want
    to see. I walk right on around
      your porch tunneled like stands
out on the road where you laid corn in double rows

and piled up the tomatoes I sold for you. I lean over
    your face boxed in ivory silk.
      You never once said *love*
or to come back here so I would see what death

will look like if death will wait this long for me.
    Maybe it's true that the dead
      return in dreams with messages
but you won't, tougher than the calluses I still can

feel on the palms of your hands. At grandma
    and grandpa's golden anniversary,
      we played blind man's bluff. *IT,*
I groped for my cousins who had already gone

back into the house. Never once telling, you let me
    search, calling to the dark, until
      I stood crying in the back field.
What can I do to get back at you, to pull the word

from your set lips that I still need to hear. A solar
    eclipse, giving no light, needing
      none, I tried to be you. Hearing
and seeing without thinking *like* or *as,* you never

looked up or back or even on when you plowed.
    Father, you had no need to label,
      certain furrowed ground would shift
from brown to green. Seeds not words planted crops.

Devil's Lane

We turn from what destroys us in time, if we can, gathering
        what can be held: my grandmother's plate
of full blown yellow and pink roses scalloped in gold. Coming
        back to take what was left of my mother's cherry
chest after the tornado outside Somerset, we found drawers

on the foundation strewn as if by thieves ignited by absence
        of money or jewels. Devil's Lane was where
we walked the summer my grandfather's farm was leveled,
        the cows sucked out as barns flew apart,
the boards lifting like souls going to heaven in Raphael's

Transfiguration. You compared our love to Natural Bridge
        we crossed the day after our wedding,
predicting we would leapfrog old laws that forbid the marriage
        of Gentile and Jew. You were the wandering
jew, a plant named not for a willing immigrant but an exile

that was impossible to kill or keep cut back like your beard.
        Clover, there was clover everywhere we
stepped and I tied stem to flower to double wreath my wrist,
        no tattoo of blue roses or numbers you could
recite from your father's arm. Picturing gloves made from baby

skin in an Israeli museum, you transformed Buchenwald and
        Belsen into a grand rounds: to experiment
with labor, a woman's feet were not raised like a mare's in
        a blacksmith's shop, but thighs strapped
together. With no exit, life was peeled from its core. Paper tigers

strung together, words couldn't metaphor those mothers, wombs
        sealed into a mausoleum. When I saw you hold

your breath in the shower, I knew you were testing how long you
    could go without breathing should the water stop.
No common boundary for the miles separating us, Germany to

Africa to Kentucky, of course I felt ethical rage. To meet your
    challenge of years I could not pull myself
through, I mouthed despair, holocaust. In time, there were fences
    like hot air that kept rising to gas I could not
breathe. Knowing what cannot be swallowed must be spit out or it

will rot like strings of meat caught between teeth, I choked on soil
    planted with your deaths. I could not block their
shadows, could not pull three sons away in time from the flames.
    If they smoldered, you fanned them to keep the fire
burning, burning through the years that can never be consumed.

Circling Above You

Like a maple seed in the pond, there is always some
        thing you have not thought of, would not
if it were not waiting for you, tail angled to sunlight.
        Look: mouth, slightly upturned, eyes green
or yellow and shaped just like two almonds swaying
        between what might be rump or shoulders.
It sticks with you like a newspaper story two summers
        ago of a snake that bit a woman's throat
while she picked beans. Avoid vegetables, the therapist
        advises. Take vitamins. Years of expense,
talk but still the fear is there, aimless. Remedies gleam,
        fool's gold streaking mine passages that
honeycomb your brain like limestone in Mammoth Cave.

Four Dollars Bought a Round Trip on the Sky Lift to the top

of Natural Bridge. One half mile, six hundred feet in altitude didn't
sound so bad, so I agreed with my father and opted for the ride.
What I'd not counted on was the trip. Proud to be saving
his eighty year old pride, I looked down on climbers sweating out

the mile. So there I was, reviewing my fear of height, as the cable
lifted us by going right up a cliff. I'd learned to get by looking
straight ahead, keeping close to earth like a copper beech. It was
sure easy to see that I couldn't do that if I used my ticket back

down. Swaying just enough in our seat, my father recited
for the fiftieth time how his brother fell from a walnut tree
being cut for cash to keep the farm because he hugged the trunk
rather than trusting ropes held to steady him. I didn't want to hear

about formations ribboning Kentucky either but I got a geology
lesson anyway on the bridge's formation. Limestone ($CaCO_3$)
was a sedimentary rock indigenous only to Florida and Kentucky.
Embedded with oceanic skeletons and peppered with aquatic

abscesses, it swelled with rain and shrunk with drought to form
sinkholes. Right before I closed my eyes for the final hawklike
ascent, my father point out the sinkhole next to a cave he climbed
down when he was nineteen since the L&N Railroad kept it strung

with electricity. Hostage to the chair's bar, I was force fed native
pride: the bridge was over seventy eight feet long; Gray's Arch
was just two feet longer and Whittleton Arch only measured
one hundred feet. Sixty years hadn't changed the mountain, just

him. I had come to find the heart I'd gouged right in the middle
of the smoothed bridge thirty years ago, the day after my wedding

in Lexington. Rock was no more lasting than my vows. The scar
my new husband and I took turns carving had worn away. Unable

to know just what day the last curve disappeared, what work boot
ground it out, all I had to touch were three sons born since I'd been
there. Turning from the edge of the bridge, I could see strength
given to me had been taken from my father but I was not about

to get back on that skyway, the two dollars per ticket and his pride
be damned! Edging down, we passed pock marked sandstone walls
I imagined in February covered with icicles, some dripping over
twenty feet high. I recited Coleridge's *Kubla Khan* with caves

of ice and sunny pleasure domes to show off how much I'd learned.
Fat Man's Misery, I told anyone who might be listening, was what
a scientist would call a vertical joint fracture with walls eighty three
feet long and fifty feet high. Looking for someone in a green park

uniform to police one way traffic, I worried about getting stuck,
swore to go on a diet. Balanced Rock developed in my solution
from a hunk of sandstone poised to spring off of its narrow stem
into a mushroom or an atomic cloud. Ignoring me, climbers turned

around to listen as my father told how the formation was known
as the Sphinx back in 1900 when the land was owned by Lexington
and Eastern Railroad. Their name had changed like mine had over
the years, first one man's, another and finally back to my father's.

Our guidebook in hand, we passed attractions one by one: old niter
mine, Devil's Gulch, Needle's Eye Stairway. As my father followed
me, I forgot the heart I had come to see, the love I believed would
form a natural bridge. Letting my father pretend he was inspecting

a piece of pipe, we paused at a large clearing, a skylight cut out by
felled trees and opened by limbs sheared in last winter's ice storm.
We argued: hemlock or pine. Remaining branches were high but
looking up at the needles that were clearly feathering, I knew how

bad his eyes must be. There was a silence I was afraid to pull like
the bit of red yarn sticking out of my sleeve. I couldn't resist
removing it from my sweater and I'd left a gaping hole. While we
both pushed up from the log bench, I explained old trees must

go to make room for new growth, how it's nature's way. There
would be no green for us. No giant spruce, my father was shedding
pounds. Surely nothing needed space he took on earth. The only
sound between us was made by the pine cones pulled down by

the earth or gnawed off and thrown by squirrels. I looked away
from those that already melted into the needled floor. I couldn't
pronounce the word *inevitable* for my father, only walk on ahead
of him over the slick parts in case he slipped and started to fall.

70

Act V, Scene iii

Chopsticks straightened, sucking orange sections, I pour our tea
and recall driving through Kentucky. Concrete bridged the road,

black paint dripping, *God lie to us*. Blessing's cookies do. I snap
dough to unthread your fortune: *Things are difficult before they*

are easy. A printed strip won't circle you like the rubber band
contracting around your father's cancer. Hook snagged in stomach,

he is trying to die but cannot let go of breath that is squeezed flat.
Stretching out for your son, clots of snow hung as he drove off,

leaving the fish tank half filled with neon tetras, a metal speaker
from an old battle ship but no note. Divorce shovels my life;

three sons will learn where their father is playing while watching
TV as I mouth words like a coach: *You can't swim in the river*

without getting wet. Sucking on red wine and the two movies
we had rented at Best Videos to analyze the impact of directing,

you puzzle over the constancy of Romeo and Juliet rather than
debating whether Laurence Harvey's dramatic display of passion

in the balcony scene erased the final act in the tomb. I try to start
an argument over the merits of casting: Castellani's use of known

stars versus Zeffirelli's unknown youths. Instead, you feast on
Juliet's last moment of steel; a love that stays, helps you through.

There Were the Signs You Had Shown Me:

I think I know enough of hate/ To say
that for destruction ice/ Is also great
ROBERT FROST

Crows gathering, birds flying low or thick fur on the bottom
    of a rabbit's foot. I know, I know. I could have
    prepared for this cold spell if I'd listened to you,
Mother. The cove at Morgan Point is snowed in. What might

be water lilies crack like the skin on your hands or scales from
    the Loch Ness monster. I could be standing by ruins
    of Urquhart castle, with thunder cutting deep through
the mountains of Scotland, but I'm in Connecticut. Three swans

with necks tucked in might be miniature icebergs, but they're not.
    Tide comes in. Pads of white slush string into lines
    of salted garland on grey water and it should be
Christmas. Packed in as I am, I will die in ice unless I regather

days of fog in August to number wintry days in December, stop
    wasting persimmons by piling them in a blue bowl.
    Slice one, I can hear you say, read the seeds: shape
of tine spoon means snow to shovel, a knife, a sharp cutting

January and a fork, a loose easy one. If all else fails, find a hornet's
    nest. High in the tree, the snow will lay on; low,
    don't unpack chains. Cut off from you down home
in Kentucky, Mother, I'm not to blame if I didn't see corn shucks

were heavy, hard to take off or ponies had extra thick coats but I do
    have a dog. Weather will be fair if the owl screeches;
    yet, all I have is gulls. I could keep charts of their flight,
live with what surrounds me, accept what has been given and what

has been taken as you taught me Papago Indians do. When water
    is scarce, their memory holds fossils of rain. Living with
    black widow spider and fire ants, none disturb kit fox
bones or step on a rattlesnake's spiral in sand, the narrow imprint

of life. Marine limestone under sand, Hohokan, ancestor of Papago,
    live even as dust, history painted on red clay that you plowed
    in Kentucky, Mother. Far from Long Island Sound, in houses
of wattle and daub, with no ice, no chinking and logs, Hohokan

wrapped women in jewels of shell, wove fine cotton to keep sand
    from skin. Learning to live in heat, they did not die from
    heat but let go, giving their bodies to the fire, their ashes
to dry wind that stirred strings of chile hotter than rust adobe walls.

Catfishing in Cumberland Lake

We have standards, won't use high powered electric lights to lure
      skater bugs and then snag the silhouettes of fish
surfacing to do an inspection. I try to explain the term *sitting*

duck to my son and why we can't go to Somerset to buy lures
      and tackle as we grab pipe cane from the bank
for a fishing pole, bend a nail into a sinker. Row out of the marina,

I order. Stop right before the mainland intersects with Burnside
      Island; we can fish where the lake begins. I wave
a fist, he gives the finger to cabin cruisers who don't obey the law

and go at throttle speed, rock us in their wake. Before putting
      a deposit on the boat, we hiked up to the falls
with a ranger who urged us to edge out onto the brink to see how

wild the river used to be. Bedrock scarred by spring floods had
      settled to silt tracked with species I couldn't trace
like the Cumberland River's path that rose in mountains of Harlan

and Letcher Counties, right near Virginia, and snaked six hundred
      and eighty seven miles to dip into the Tennessee,
gouging a channel right up to where we stood. Floating on the lake,

our lines drifting, I stop the science lectures and start to unwind.
      The ridges and bluffs make it easy to forget
the laurel, the cedar drowning as Wolf Creek Dam was opened.

According to a picture in the lodge, it took one man in a green park
      shirt to open the gate and to turn the sky loose.
Water racing, foaming at the mouth swallowed the valley whole.

Stands of slow growing scrub pine that had survived every drought
      would surely have flown in panic if branches

were feathered not thorned to hold fast. Nothing winged, no black

and red woodpecker to tap dance a rhythm on a dead trunk, the next
    morning is still. My son and I are sitting on the shore
since I had to return the boat the night before even though neither

of us caught a fish. He blames me for my inexperience, for being
    born a woman, not being his father who'd know
tricks like spitting on a worm before throwing it in and how to bait

our hooks with dough balls or offal. It's useless to explain that half
    a day's rental costs almost as much as a full one
and the support check from his father hasn't come for two months.

My son scatters blame like blowing the head off a dandelion.
    Under the lake's dark skin, fish must be hiding
from us in grass, under roots that will never know rain, clay that

will never dry into hardtack but on the bank, only black ants move.
    Too bad the weeds keep blocking our view
because my son would have enjoyed their struggle during the six

hours we had to kill before the next bus. Passing the time, we pile
    a monument of snail shells shaped like white
helmets his grandfather had worn in the Boer War. Finally, we snag

a catfish and my son agrees to go home only on one condition — he
    gets to carry our catch back alive in a cardboard
KFC bucket I'd saved from supper. Our trophy stayed by the side

door for days, shaded by canvas torn off a deck chair. Saturday
    morning, getting ready for the trip to the dump,
I lifted the body with a broom handle even though there was no rot

no odor, no wound. To ease my son's guilt over an unkept promise,
    I could have pictured how death would have come
in the lake: mites in pits of what were lidless eyes; a wide grinning

mouth that would eat anything now open to leeches; intestines like
      bleached rubber bands cut in half swaying
with green and bronzed flies. I'm afraid he won't sleep through

the whole night and so I field his questions on the catfish's soul,
      if flying would be like swimming, gills for wings.
What is awkward in air like passion has a grace in water but grace

can vanish like his father's desire for me did and I urge him not to
      think about what it's impossible to know: do
catfish big as men, as big as Jaws, lurk submerged in mud waiting

at the base of the dam? What is gone, is gone like our family
      or stripped like limbs of old elms rising as if
lifting arms to heaven. But I do want him to remember this August

day we floated over the floor of Cumberland Lake not thinking
      of the drowned valley but of how driftwood
settled. Spelling each other, we rowed an hour to find the right

inlet to drop our anchor. My son pointed to water as it changed
      color with the shifting of the sun, folded rock,
algae oozing like glue balls, the chimneys of crayfish. Grateful for

water more accessible than feeder creeks deep in hollows, we could
      see that when one shore closed, the lake began
to open another one, hinting at yet another one beyond every bend.

No Six Pounders

Sprays of sea grass yanked out to clear the sand,
beach is rushing to new growth. One legged weed
in shallows, a white heron passes time, the aim
of its bill more accurate than my son's hook.
After he was born, I was an ear each night, fearful
his breathing would stop but sleep has come back
into my summer like dark does, always catching
me by surprise. A cormorant dives making a wake
in slate faced water. A scar healing, the surface
closes over what swims beneath as I try to distract
my son, keep him from repeating the question I
pretend I don't hear. I explain that the cormorant
has webbed toes, a hooked beak and an appetite
for snappers that can't be filled. As I describe
how fishermen in China double knot a silken rope
around one leg, using the leashed bird to catch fish,
my son interrupts to ask why his father doesn't call,
doesn't visit or bring his boat to take him fishing.

Satisfied with my answers, distracted by the bobber,
his bait is swallowed by huge striped bass we imagine
but never catch. At the filling station, pictures of men
holding up blues are our lures. Mounted jaws of sharks
caught off the rocks at Morgan Point keep us casting
and casting. My son is sure that if his father were here,
we would catch fish after fish and he waves to every boat
that passes just in case it might be him after all. To pass
the time, we use a coffee can to trap a crab, then another.
Again, there are questions about why his father hunts
but won't fish and others I can't answer — why lobsters
turn red when boiled or the difference in deaths,
our fishing unlike bullets killing a fox, body discarded,
tail snipped for the Harley his father has bought to ride.

Unnatural

Once the Valedictorian, now the father, you flinched
as Eric flapped the stage, earring and sunglasses glinting
while his name, not the same as yours, melted into another.
The question had become no longer one of rank at graduation
but of a degree; four years taken from you could not be
regathered like the apples from a basket he smashed.
Marrying his mother, moving his *Grateful Dead* posters
like leftovers from a tag sale, you gave him the chance
to reinvent himself. Your sentences scraped nothing,
not even membranes of his sleep. With a pillow over his eyes,
was he laughing at you during the daily morning lies you told,
the notes you wrote for his body that would not get out of bed,
the explanations you created for holes his fist put in doors?
Did fighting ease his anger, or was it that younger brothers were
outside listening to Eric numb you with *fuck this, fuck that?*

Guns and Roses, Pink Floyd or *AC/DC* blasted through
on CD's you had paid for, on speakers too large, too heavy
to be hung from chains anchored to the ceiling. *Nirvana*
gave him the words: *chokin' on the ashes; all we know
is all we are.* Teaching you that it wasn't just sticks and stones
but words that could still hurt you, he'd hurl, *Jagger's old,
just like you, Dude. Both of you should've packed it in before
you hit thirty, showed some real class and pulled a Cobain.*

Guilt had grown stale like water standing too long in a glass.
Too much about injustice, the divorce. Too much bailing
water from a ship, holes left by the father, the natural father,
he would never find. How could you speak of the man? *Step*
was the salt he rubbed on your skin each day. After he spit
in your face, you learned how unnatural this son, love could be.

No smile or thumb up in your camera's direction when he waved
the diploma aloft, the only sign Eric gave to you was a turning,

the way a leaf must to the sun. Grafted, the new life had not taken. After the ceremony, you went to The Chowder Pot to celebrate. He punched rocks into water as if Long Island Sound could be filled with stone. If the two of you had been on either end of a boat separated by mist and not blood, this son, this unnatural son, knew he wouldn't have needed to call out your name but could sit waiting for the slushing of your oars. No sextant, nothing was left for you but to hold steady, rowing blind in a fog that might not lift.

Night Fishing at Morgan Point

Weighted down by frozen bait, insurance
that my son and I would never need lures,
we were linked by ritual of hook and rod.

Matthew had dipped into schools of kellys;
to show him how to secure one still alive
by pushing steel through middle, I pictured

the blue heron his brother had nicknamed
Doctor Doom for the aim of its bill.
Cradling his hands, I wanted to tell him how

I held him on the ride home just a day
after he was born, how his mother and I
drank champagne, making love on the sand

at Morgan Point the night he was conceived,
how I packed her suitcase before rushing her
to the hospital, filling her room with roses,

how I watched his head emerge. None of this
happened. No priest consecrating bread
and wine to place the Eucharist in outstretched

hands and tongues, I could not perform
a sacrament transfusing my love into his blood.
I would have a beer before settling down to wait

the arcing of the line flung out over the moon.
A shining whipped the night, hung like a shred
before my son reeled in the snapper. Lashing

the dark, we would cast into unfamiliar depths,
until we snagged another then another. Our talk
was of stars and not why Matthew at fifteen

had become inscrutable to me. I could not speak
of my fear that he would find my ordinary life,
my love, lacked luster in the telling light. Instead,

I told him that he must gut the fish he catches
so it does not rot and taught him how to hold
a knife as he cut the fillets for us to grill. Later,

beginning our own tradition, we fed one another
the first bite from the fish we had caught, from
the meal we had created, from the flesh we shared.

No Ark

I've counted seven days of rain. Are the halcyon days gone south
of the equator along with the sun? I know all about December 21st,
the winter solstice, but it's too early for night, for closure, too late
to practice *Jesu Christi*, my baritone entry in Verdi's *Requiem*.

Jesu Christi, Jesu Christi! I need daffodils not withered seeds
on bent grey stalks. The garden's Swiss chard. Perennial design,
plan, pattern, where is it? Already Thursday, how can I write
with thoughts of my body that could break clean as a peony stem
and then the dirt closing around me like dough kneaded for biscuit?

There's been no deep cold. I'll buy bone meal half price. Planting
will become my metaphor — bulbs for faith, the ice that can glide me
over January and February even though I know statistics: moles
who feast on tulips or a cancer that can out trumpet King Alfred.

April will burst with narcissus, borders of collars, flatcups, tazettas.
March can be oriental, carpeted in crocus of Goldilocks, Lady Killer,
Little Dorrit, Peter Pan. I'll fax an express to White Flower Farms:
ten dozen double nosed bulbs guaranteed to perform the first year.

To defy at least moles, I can line the walk with tulips chosen
for names: Johann Strauss, Elizabeth Arden, General Eisenhower.
No Madonna lilies massed on an altar for me! In June, there will be
Casa Blanca; in July, Strawberry Shortcake, white and crimson.
To float me through August's heat, I'll position liliums in a parade
of petals flooding a path: pearls, golds, bronzes, coppers and rubies.

Horse Breath Winter

I won't die looking like you. An old black walnut, thick shelled
with shrunken meat, you are too small to hide underground.
Grandma, on Saturday nights when it was so cold we didn't ride

into town, I had to brush off cake flour that clung to your face
like snow shrouding wood I chopped and then stacked. Leaning
on the door frame for support, you'd beat time on the bowl

of brown sugar frosting while I took turns with my cousins
cranking the victrola. We danced, careful not to fingerprint
the blue velvet parlor sofa where you let grandpa rest up

after washing for supper. You're not even a ghost yet. Unable
to swing my grief like a child between us, I can't stroke
your skin, transparent as waxed paper pressing a veined leaf.

Pulling away from you, I remember how scared I was when
you made me run across the swinging bridge. You weren't afraid
to get wet or of the water moccasins I had seen swimming.

When they crawled up for the warmth between the kitchen
boards and red flowered wallpaper, you chopped them in half
with the hoe and put up a new pattern, happy, you said,

to have an excuse to give grandpa for the blue striped pattern
you'd had your eye on. Trying to smooth in white cold cream
that will not sink through the veins knotted around your hands,

I picture rocks slicked with strings of moss rising in the bed
of Rough Creek during a drought. Dried out, the stones rose up
to line a path I could jump, slipping right across to the other side.

Stony Creek Granite

Unexpected, this day melting
winter, seasons still locked
within the ground. *False Spring,*
you call out to me while I watch you
rebuild walls, bind your land
with thriftiness of line. The top
is already spilling over the earth;
other rocks flatten, bend down as if
yearning to avalanche hollows. Rehearsed
in lifting gravity, knowing the earth
does not repent of stones, you wedge
granite worn to pink not speckled grey
like the photograph of my father
and you, two brothers, standing
at the bottom of the Statue of Liberty.

You never tire of pulling the picture
from your wallet and talking about
the statue's base, how it's built
of this same pink Stony Creek granite.
Your grandfather quarried it, blasting
sections to cut for engineers with charts,
fortification against frost that heaves
earth, the boulders for your numbed hands
to pry. Odd, you say, the tension in unhewn.
unmarked stone. There is no final resting.

I'll leave you here until morning, Uncle.
You don't want to end this spring ritual
that's like putting out a leaking pan
to catch rain water for my hair. I'll be back
tomorrow and again I'll wonder if you think
of the wall against snow, muffled in grass

or how the earth moves like water. Sunset
is the good hour for you, spent watching
hawks float, never measuring the days in hours
taken to tie stalks of corn as my father does.
I see you gaze skyward, appearing to measure
fields out of your reach. Or are you looking up
to stones for light to guide you through?

Soon, Soon,

my son would whisper as I imagined netting dark
    not bait darting into tide pool moss.
        Twilight was best with shadows

crossing and uncrossing like legs of cheerleaders
    seated on bleachers at a home game.
        Pickle jar, insurance against

lures, Matt scooped kellys but I hooked them,
    fearing for his thumb. Brushing sand
        lice from my knees and thighs,

I'd lecture myself, *There is a limit*. When the blue
    struck, I turned away knowing what
        I would have to do, that he

was still too young to handle a knife. Fingers wrestling
    the insides, guts over my wrist,
        I was grateful no sun gleamed

in the fish's eye. Rubbing the knuckle of my index finger
    under my nose, a habit I couldn't break,
        I'd inhale the smell for days.

Like squid left to dry that curl and stick to the deck rail,
    cleaned scales fell to silver the grass.
        Staying put through winter,

they papered asphalt washed by spring rain, glittered
    then rolled into blue flesh leaping off
        the hook, resurrected from my hands.

The Stepfather

Do years add layers as silt does, filtering down through a river
flowing quietly, sure of its direction as we have been for fourteen

years? There was no ritual for becoming a family when I married
your mother. Our three last names even stayed separate, were not

blended into one word we could stencil on the mailbox. I did not
understand your mother's anger at the years she could not erase

by removing monograms from silver or by changing your initials
to her own. At times, her rage was a fire, scorching all the ground

around us. Peace like the dandelions we dug out year after year,
jagged spears of green spreading out to carpets of yellow, crept in

pushing back the blackness farther and farther until one day it was
faint, a ring surrounding us and then it was our memory. Because it

is easy, the metaphor of planting comes readily. So common but
I cannot think of another comparison that would not be contrived,

that would be natural for a stepfather's love that is not. What
I did not seed, I can harvest; the earth has been deeded to me.

Yet, as I stand at Sachem Field waiting behind the soccer posts,
I sometimes fall silent, not screaming out *Yes!* as other fathers do

when their sons score a goal. Another man's name being broadcast
over the P.A. system slaps my ears. At the fall sports banquet,

after being picked all conference and MVP, you called me up
to the podium. While we stood posing for the *North Haven Post*,

need to see my name engraved on you for a plaque I could mount
in the hall fell from my heart. With no words in our vocabulary

for *blood,* *own,* or *real,* we each grasped a handle; there was no
step or hyphen labeling the love bridging us, the trophy we shared.